# City of a Hundred Fires

*1997 Agnes Lynch Starrett Poetry Prize*

*Pitt Poetry Series*

Ed Ochester, *Editor*

# City of a Hundred Fires

## Richard Blanco

University of Pittsburgh Press

Published by the University of Pittsburgh Press, Pittsburgh, Pa. 15261

Manufactured in the United States of America

Printed on acid-free paper

10 9 8 7 6 5 4 3 2 1

Art on page ii: Carlos Betancourt.

Acknowledgments are located at the end of this book.

A CIP catalog record for this book is available from the Library of Congress and the British Library.

*The publication of this book is supported by a grant from the Pennsylvania Council on the Arts.*

In loving memory of my father, and his memories.

*En memoria de mi padre, y sus recuerdos.*

Carlos Emilio Blanco

1935–1990

# Contents / Indice

**I**

América   3

Teatro Martí   7

La Revolución at Antonio's Mercado   8

Mango, Number 61   10

El Malibú   11

Islamorada   12

Crayons for Elena   13

Mail for Mamá   14

Los Santos of the Living Room   15

Mother Picking Produce   16

The Lesson   17

Shaving   19

Letter to El Flaco on His Birthday   21

Hola   23

324 Mendoza Avenue, #6   24

What Las Palmas Mean:   26

La Bella Dama of Little Havana   28

A Note About Sake   29

The Silver Sands   30

Photo Shop   31

Contemplations at the Virgin de la Caridad Cafetería, Inc.   33

# II

Havanasis   37

Varadero en Alba   39

The Road to Rancho Luna   41

Havana 50s   42

El Jagua Resort   43

Last Night in Havana   46

El Juan   48

Partial List: Guantánamo Detainees   49

Found Letters from 1965: El Año de la Agricultura   50

The Reservoir   55

Abuela Valdés   57

El Cucubano   59

Zafra   61

The Morning Kill   62

Tía Olivia Serves Wallace Stevens a Cuban Egg   64

Décima Guajira   66

Postcard to W. C. Williams from Cienfuegos   67

Palmita Mía   68

Palmita Mía (translation)   70


Acknowledgments / Agradecimientos   73

I'll see in my mind's eye:
  it's entitled to go where I cannot,
can freewheel over enormous distances, reaches
  heaven in its swift course, conveys my eyes
to the heart of the City.

    Ovid, *The Poems of Exile;* translated into English by Peter Green


*Veré en los ojos de la imaginación:*
  *tiene el derecho de ir donde yo no puedo,*
*puede recorrer enormes distancias, alcanza*
  *el cielo en su curso veloz, lleva mis ojos*
*al corazón de la Ciudad.*

    Ovid, *Los Poemas del Exilio;* translated into Spanish from English by Richard Blanco

# América

**I.**

Although Tía Miriam boasted she discovered
at least half a dozen uses for peanut butter—
topping for guava shells in syrup,
butter substitute for Cuban toast,
hair conditioner and relaxer—
*Mamá* never knew what to make
of the monthly five-pound jars
handed out by the immigration department
until my friend, Jeff, mentioned jelly.

**II.**

There was always pork though,
for every birthday and wedding,
whole ones on Christmas and New Year's Eve,
even on Thanksgiving day—pork,
fried, broiled, or crispy skin roasted—
as well as cauldrons of black beans,
fried plantain chips, and *yuca con mojito*.
These items required a special visit
to Antonio's Mercado on the corner of Eighth Street
where men in *guayaberas* stood in senate
blaming Kennedy for everything—*"Ese hijo de puta!"*
the bile of Cuban coffee and cigar residue
filling the creases of their wrinkled lips;
clinging to one another's lies of lost wealth,
ashamed and empty as hollow trees.

## III.

By seven I had grown suspicious—we were still here.
Overheard conversations about returning
had grown wistful and less frequent.
I spoke English; my parents didn't.
We didn't live in a two-story house
with a maid or a wood-panel station wagon
nor vacation camping in Colorado.
None of the girls had hair of gold;
none of my brothers or cousins
were named Greg, Peter, or Marcia;
we were not the Brady Bunch.
None of the black and white characters
on Donna Reed or on the Dick Van Dyke Show
were named Guadalupe, Lázaro, or Mercedes.
Patty Duke's family wasn't like us either—
they didn't have pork on Thanksgiving,
they ate turkey with cranberry sauce;
they didn't have *yuca,* they had yams
like the dittos of Pilgrims I colored in class.

## IV.

A week before Thanksgiving
I explained to my *abuelita*
about the Indians and the Mayflower,
how Lincoln set the slaves free;
I explained to my parents about
the purple mountain's majesty,
"one if by land, two if by sea,"
the cherry tree, the tea party,

the amber waves of grain,
the "masses yearning to be free,"
liberty and justice for all, until
finally they agreed:
this Thanksgiving we would have turkey,
as well as pork.

## U.

*Abuelita* prepared the poor fowl
as if committing an act of treason,
faking her enthusiasm for my sake.
*Mamá* set a frozen pumpkin pie in the oven
and prepared candied yams following instructions
I translated from the marshmallow bag.
The table was arrayed with gladiolas,
the plattered turkey loomed at the center
on plastic silver from Woolworth's.
Everyone sat in green velvet chairs
we had upholstered with clear vinyl,
except Tío Carlos and Toti, seated
in the folding chairs from the Salvation Army.
I uttered a bilingual blessing
and the turkey was passed around
like a game of Russian Roulette.
"DRY," Tío Berto complained, and proceeded
to drown the lean slices with pork fat drippings
and cranberry jelly—*"esa mierda roja,"* he called it.
Faces fell when *Mamá* presented her ochre pie—
pumpkin was a home remedy for ulcers, not a dessert.
Tía María made three rounds of Cuban coffee

then *Abuelo* and Pepe cleared the living room furniture,
put on a Celia Cruz LP and the entire family
began to *merengue* over the linoleum of our apartment,
sweating rum and coffee until they remembered—
it was 1970 and 46 degrees—
in *América*.
After repositioning the furniture,
an appropriate darkness filled the room.
Tío Berto was the last to leave.

# Teatro Martí

Outside, I would close one eye and squint the other and count the bulbs in English while everyone stood for tickets. Inside Sarita Montiel awaited without subtitles. Always the semi-nude scene: Sarita in her porous eggshell skin, a perfect sienna mole, eyebrows penciled like Japanese ink strokes on silk, the soft balls of her feet and strawberry toenails seeping from under the edges of sheets swirled around her contours like icing, propped on her breasts and elbows and crying with a *Gallego* lisp into a gross of satin pillows, believing there would be justice for her undeserved suffering. Justice because she loved; simply because she loved. We believed what she believed because there was little to trust in, and so much to remember in 1972, and no place else to pretend on Saturday nights. Hovering in the dark, nestled in cracked vinyl seats, silently in our row, we conjured our own justice, in spite of ourselves and our losses. While we ate smuggled *coquitos* and *cremitas de leche,* outside the fifty-eight frosted bulbs would flash in unison bursts of mint-white, like a beacon, on-off, on-off, signaling the '72 Malibus and the '67 Chevys whizzing by on Eighth Street to come in and wake us from the slow annihilation we pretended to ignore each Saturday and each day since *la Revolución,* and to save us, too.

# La Revolución at Antonio's Mercado

*Para la santera,* Esperanza, who makes me open new boxes of candles so she
can pick out the red ones, the color of *Changó,* her protector spirit, and
tutors me in the ways of all the spirits: *Eleguá, Ochún, Yemayá,*

*Para* Josie on welfare, who sells me her food stamps for cash because she can't
buy cocoa butter soaps, Coca-Cola, or disposable diapers with them,

*Para la* Señora Vidal and her husband who came early in the 50s before *la Rev-
olución,* own the famous Matador Grille on Eighth Street, helped those
who came later, who give me two-dollar tips when I double bag,

*Para* Elena who makes me sort through cartfuls of avocados to find the *best*
one, her nostalgia-coated tongue complains that the fruit here can't com-
pare to the fruit back home—where the sugar was sweeter, the salt saltier,

*Para* Juan Galdo who remains unsatisfied with the flavor of *los tabacos de Hon-
duras,*

*Para* Mrs. Benitez the only regular who buys broccoli, who takes English
night class and asks me to check her homework,

*Para* Pepe who asks me to translate his insurance statements, immigration pa-
pers, and junk mail offers for "free" vacations in Mexico,

*Para* the cashier, Consuelo, who wants me to teach her daughter, María, Eng-
lish and love, and wants me to escort María to her *Quinces* debutante,

*Para* Migdalia Sanchez who forgets some labels are now bilingual and comes
to me confused when she mistakenly tries to read the English side of the
can,

*Para la vieja* Gomez who I help sort through dimes, quarters, and nickels—
American change she has never learned to count,

*Para los americanos* who are scared of us, especially when we talk real loud and
all at the same time, who come in only for change or to call a tow truck,

*Para los haitianos* who like us because at least we are Caribbean neighbors,

*Para* Pablito who likes his boiled ham sliced paper-thin like the after-school snacks his mother prepared for him before she was accused and sentenced,

*Para* Juanita who had to leave Enrique, her only son, in '61, who carries in her sequined coin purse a scratchy photo of herself at fifteen to remind herself she is still alive, and shows it to me so I can acknowledge her lost beauty,

*Para* Carlos who comes in mid-mornings, leans against the cafeteria counter drunk with delusion, takes a swig of espresso like a shot of whiskey and tells me *la Revolución* will die before the end of the year, who hopes to host *Noche Buena* at his house near Havana, next year,

*Para la Revolución, todos sus grandes triunfos, toda su gloria,*

*Para* Vicente my best friend, who sneaked beers with me behind the green Dumpster, who taught me how to say really gross things in Spanish, who couldn't get his family out, who had only me in the States, who put a bullet through his neck on the day of his anniversary, who left a note addressed to me in Spanish—*"Para mi amigo."*

## Mango, Number 61

*Pescado grande* was number 14, while *pescado chico* was number 12; *dinero,* money, was number 10. This was *la charada,* the sacred and obsessive numerology my *abuela* used to predict lottery numbers or winning trifectas at the dog track. The grocery stores and pawn shops on Flagler Street handed out complimentary wallet-size cards printed with the entire *charada,* numbers 1 through 100: number 70 was *coco,* number 89 was *melón,* and number 61 was *mango.* Mango was Mrs. Pike, the last *americana* on the block with the best mango tree in the neighborhood. *Mamá* would coerce her in granting us picking rights—after all, *los americanos don't eat mango,* she'd reason. Mango was fruit wrapped in brown paper bags, hidden like ripening secrets in the kitchen oven. Mango was the perfect housewarming gift and a marmalade dessert with thick slices of cream cheese at birthday dinners and Thanksgiving. Mangos, watching like amber cat's eyes. Mangos, perfectly still in their speckled maroon shells like giant unhatched eggs. Number 48 was *cucaracha,* number 36 was *bodega,* but mango was my uncle's *bodega,* where everyone spoke only loud Spanish, the precious gold fruit towering in *tres-por-un-peso* pyramids. Mango was mango shakes made with milk, sugar and a pinch of salt—my grandfather's treat at the Eighth Street market after baseball practice. Number 60 was *sol,* number 18 was *palma,* but mango was my father and I under the largest shade tree at the edges of Tamiami park. Mango was *Abuela* and I hunched over the counter covered with the Spanish newspaper, devouring the dissected flesh of the fruit slithering like molten gold through our fingers, the nectar cascading from our binging chins, *Abuela* consumed in her rapture and convinced that I absolutely loved mangos. Those messy mangos. Number 79 was *cubano*—us, and number 93 was *revolución,* though I always thought it should be 58, the actual year of the revolution—the reason why, I'm told, we live so obsessively and nostalgically eating number 61's, *mangos,* here in number 87, *América.*

# El Malibú

*Papá* smelled of fine *tabaco* and the dried blood
stains on his pants and underneath the fingernails
of his tender and pink meat-locker hands.
After four years as head butcher at *el mercado,*
he saved enough cash for a deal on a '72 Malibu,
two door, plush vinyl, with FM and lighter,
eight-track tape player under the driver's seat.

We rode in style that first summer vacation,
the copper-brown metallic finish of *el Malibú*
glimmering over turnpike tarmac and grove hills,
eight tracks of melancholy boleros playing
through cypress swamps and billboard holler
on a whirlwind of motel pools and theme parks:
goldfish worlds under glass-bottom boats,
enchanted castles, fireworks, and roller coasters,
water-ski pyramids of bathing caps and ruffles,
reenactments of Wild, Wild West shoot-outs.

Cruising our new country in our new car,
through attractions and distractions, convinced
we'd made it so many years since *la Revolución*—
*Papá* held to his leather-wrapped steering wheel
like a worn matador to red wine, denying loss,
denying the scented hills remind him of his hills—
his hands clean and manicured, free of blood.

## Islamorada

Nets like cobwebs to the sea then he speaks
to the other sardine fishermen on the pier.
I lean like a sail to capture his voice, fill
with the wind from a distant 1940s Cuba.

Nets open and wet the pier, we gather
the silvery spill of bodies, through our hands
into buckets where they quiver for a while
then die above the lapping of waves.

The day ebbs into dusk, the sand thickens,
we fold the nets under the early stars,
then retreat from the sea as the tide turns,
our hands full, our mouths empty.

# Crayons for Elena

This is for the $1.98 flip-top box of crayons we buried in my mother's shopping cart and coerced her into buying for us; how we capitalized on sympathy and the pitying looks of the cashier and customers behind us, embarrassed her at the checkout with our *fuchsia* pleas until she gave in. This is for the thunderstorms and the after-school afternoons—cartoons rioting in the screened Florida room while we sprawled on the floor and warmed the cold tile, tested all sixty-four crayons on junk mail scraps and blank newsprint. Even the colors we didn't understand—*sienna brown, peach,* and *white*—the ones that reminded us of freckled Brian, the only *americano* in the fourth grade. And the colors that thrilled us—the dangling live lizards from our earlobes colors—*pink, jungle green;* the mango slices and *mamey* flesh colors—*gold, raspberry;* the double-butter popcorn on a Saturday matinee colors—*silver, periwinkle;* the burst *la piñata* colors—*lemon-yellow, cornflower-blue;* the we don't know English colors—*chartreuse, cerulean.* All these we wore down to stubs, peeling the paper coating further and further, peeling and sharpening until eventually we removed the color's name. This is for leaving the box in the back seat of my father's new *copper* Malibu, the melted collage, the butter knife we used to scrape the seat, and the scent of wax. For all the color in our lives that still confuses and delights us.

## Mail for Mamá

For years they have come for you:
awkward-size envelopes labeled POR AVION
affixed with multiple oversized stamps
honoring men from that other country.

Monthly, you would peel eggshell pages,
the white onionskin paper telling details:
Kiki's first steps, your mother's death,
dates approximated by the postmarks.

Sometimes with pictures: mute black-and-whites,
poor photos of poor cousins I would handle
looking for my resemblance in the foreign
image of an ear, an eyebrow, or a nose.

When possible, you would parcel a few pounds
of your desperation in discreet brown packages:
medicines, bubble gum, our family's photos,
a few yards of taffeta needed for a *Quinces* gown.

Always waiting for your letters, your face worn
like the coral face of a water fountain goddess—
your mouth of stone, your eyes forever fixed
by a sentence of time, in a garden of never.

# Los Santos of the Living Room

At her *Quinces* ball, my cousin Susana was presented to society as a lavish pearl, unveiled from a giant enameled oyster rolled right into the center of the festivities. The commemorative portrait of the fifteen-year-old debutante—caped in feathers, coyly posed with cherubs at her feet on the marble staircases of Vizcaya Palace and wisping an Andalucian fan—hung conspicuously in our living room, competing with the velvet furniture, the avocado marquise curtains and crême chiffon sheers. *Mamá* also hung flea market oil paintings of palm tree landscapes and ink sketches of La Habana Vieja—La Catedral, El Capitolio, El Morro. In the china cabinet: souvenir plates and toothpick holders from Niagara Falls, a miniature Flamenco doll with authentic ivory comb and stomping shoes, fine porcelain espresso *tacitas* with etched vine roses used only for high entertaining, a few genuine Lladró figurines glazed in trademark shades of strict gray-blues, and *los santos:*

*Santa Bárbara,* 14 inches high with a gold-plated chalice and halo, a spade in her right hand ready to lance evil, mounted sidesaddle on her majestic horse; *San Lázaro* the crippled leper, glassy eyed, caped in purple velvet, the wire armature showing through broken-off fingers and toes; and the patron of the homeland—*La Virgen de la Caridad del Cobre*—floating above a mystic sea, protecting our island. *Mamá* insisted we are not *santero* pagans despite the votive candles and the offerings of glossy apples, the glassfuls of water, the bowls of hard candies and copper pennies I would steal from the saints, and the lit *tabaco* smoke swirling with prayer: *Santa Bárbara bendita, san velvet, san chiffon, Our Lady of the Oyster, Santa Susana de las Quinceñeras, santos del Flamenco fire, Holy Havana, San Lladró y santísimo San Lázaro, santos del café, sweet saints of the cane, royal santos of las palmas, bendito San Nostalgia, spirit of our fathers and protector of our perpetual dreaming—pray for us, save us, deliver us, return us.*

## Mother Picking Produce

She scratches the oranges then smells the peel,
presses an avocado just enough to judge its ripeness,
polishes the Macintoshes searching for bruises.

She selects with hands that have thickened, fingers
that have swollen with history around the white gold
of a wedding ring she now wears as a widow.

Unlike the archived photos of young, slender digits
captive around black and white orange blossoms,
her spotted hands now reaching into the colors.

I see all the folklore of her childhood, the fields,
the fruit she once picked from the very tree,
the wiry roots she pulled out of the very ground.

And now, among the collapsed boxes of *yuca,*
through crumbling pyramids of golden mangos,
she moves with the same instinct and skill.

This is how she survives death and her son,
on these humble duties that will never change,
on those habits of living which keep a life a life.

She holds up red grapes to ask me what I think,
and what I think is this, a new poem about her—
the grapes look like dusty rubies in her hands,

what I say is this: *they look sweet, very sweet.*

# The Lesson

I am being eight again. We are in the shadeless backyard,
and *Papá* lands a marvelous blow between the fixed eyes
with the blunt end of a weapon. I can't remember the weapon—
a blunt piece of 2x4 perhaps, say it is a scrap length of pipe
and say the loosened clumps of the rabbit's massless hairs
float lethargically, suspended in the air of that warm autumn,
then sift through the open screens into the Florida room.
Say they parachute down like the most papery of leaves
swaying in midair and land camouflaged on the white tile,
until *Mamá* takes a slow broom patiently across the floor.

He cuts a slit the width of an eye in the manifold of skin
at the short neck, right below the jaw, and the white fur
is drenched by the crude red as quickly as a cotton ball.
He seals the slit with his full lips, then blows into the limp animal,
his cheeks strain, the blood seeps from the edges of his mouth,
and I can't remember the color, say it was like red mercury
and it rolls slick over his bronze cheek and drips off his chin
on the blades of green grass, and say those were emerald.

The animal swells and the fur detaches from the flesh as it should,
and he says proudly: *This is how it's done! Como un hombre!*
What was he remembering—the memory of his exile courage:
mountain trails, barefoot country, and cockfights now lost.
I don't know. I know *Papá* narrates the butchering, a gentle voice
shows me how to stretch the souvenir pelt out in the sun to dry.
What was the lesson, say it was a unique metaphor for what now
I understand as the necessity of killing beyond human wishes,
the very instincts that drive me to consume even what I love.

When the quartering is done, *Mamá* is already in the kitchen

sizzling cumin, garlic, and laurel leaves in *vino seco* and olive oil
in her preferred black *cazuela* over the iridescent gas stove.
She cuts the flame to tend the scratches on *Papá's* forearms
with sun-dried washcloths, alcohol, and a mercurochrome
which stains his silent skin an antiseptic orange for days.
And I know I may never remember that exact color either,
say, cool-fire, the orange of an impressionist sun rising.

## Shaving

I am not shaving, I'm writing about it.
And I conjure the most elaborate idea—
how my beard is a creation of silent labor
like ocean steam rising to form clouds,
or the bloom of spiderwebs each morning;
the discrete mystery of how whiskers grow,
like the drink roses take from the vase,
or the fall of fresh rain, becoming
a river, and then rain again, so silently.
I think of all these slow and silent forces
and how quietly my father's life passed us by.

I think of those mornings, when I *am* shaving,
and remember him in a masquerade of foam, then,
as if it was his beard I took the blade to,
the memory of him in tiny snips of black whiskers
swirling in the drain—dead pieces of the self
from the face that never taught me how to shave.
His legacy of whiskers that grow like black seeds
sown over my cheek and chin, my own flesh.

I am not shaving, but I will tell you about the mornings
with a full beard and the blade in my hand,
when my eyes don't recognize themselves
in a mirror echoed with a hundred faces
I have washed and shaved—it is in that split second,
when perhaps the roses drink and the clouds form,

when perhaps the spider spins and rain transforms,
that I most understand the invisibility of life
and the intensity of vanishing, like steam
at the slick edges of the mirror, without a trace.

## Letter to El Flaco on His Birthday

Querido Flaco,

The ride was cool, wasn't it? Us five
modern Spartans on a rampage in Zamar's '67 Olds,
heavy solid steel doors that slammed like traps,
neat triangular window slits drawing in the rushing wind,
a new paint job the color of a clear-blue breath mint,
itchy foam oozing from gashed seats,
the smell of monoxides and cigarettes
as familiar and engulfing as memories of fathers
and Saturday mornings spent learning how to drive.
We've learned how to drive, we've driven:
to work where we park our lives behind mahogany,
to classroom ideals or to nickel-beer joints;
through stokes of rain and the warping light
of unattempted allies that swallow city rapture
the way black holes take in starlight.
All those miles. All the books we've read—
of poetry and philosophy, of art and architecture—
and still we can't decide whether to burn recklessly
or become simple verses of ethics and obligation.

Today, the road led to the Pink Pussycat,
we strapped dollar bills in the lace garters
of our mothers and our sisters (not-dancing),
of our future wives and unborn daughters (not-dancing),
wiggling around brass posts like licorice,

as we stood ready to evaporate in the heat
of the flashing bulbs that trimmed the stage.
Did you think of da Vinci or Dante, did you decide
between glances at Rita's brown-nippled breasts
*jelloing* side-to-side above the mirrored stool. Don't.
Instead, count the sprinkled late night drives, the road
a slippery winding of eel skin, reflecting, if not stars,
the equally spaced cinnamon haloes of luminaries
guiding you home to those empty rooms you fill
with the pulse of *bembés* pulled from Tito's bongo,
the African gods hibernating in your black forest eyelashes,
the heartfuls of musical orgy from Mulata's studio
where you've thrown off your suede bucks
and learned how to dance like a Salsa King,
in the stairwell of a four-story walk-up.

Don't think of Nietzsche or Eliot. Don't decide.
Today think of the finite number of midnight runs
for pizza or nachos, drive-thrus and one last smoke;
the times you fill the gas tank for the ride home,
the traffic lights stop flashing, begin their steady burn,
and the night closes a cappella in a song all our own.

## Hola

A saving quarter from a linted pocket, a week-old number on a napkin I had by now memorized like the taste of water. I dial you. My voice crackling with the static of the pay phone. You answer the Sunday call with *"hola,"* a homonym for wave—*ola*—in our language of silent *h*'s and a silent beach where we meet as if we could resolve something; as if by staring at the vastness of the universe icing the Atlantic anything could become less important by contrast. Tonight Gemini is two fireflies hovering about my fingertip and I could be Polaris, a moon or a grain of sand just the same. I have little defense against all this paradox. I could easily finish drowning tonight in the throat of waves, let their foamy mouths seal me in a sepulcher of coral. Or I could fuse with the fine quartz descending in your green eyes, become a small dune in your palm and drown instead in the *hola* of your greeting, your Spanish voice that is a guitar strumming chestfuls of black heartbeats, pulling waves from the obsidian of night and sea. Tonight, I sleep with the taste of your salt, with a grit in my teeth.

## 324 Mendoza Avenue, #6

The last time I drank vodka, I drank it straight, in that chair.
You played Streisand from her famous concert in Central Park,
in '72, you said, and handed me the album cover which folded out.
I read the gloss and statistics, "largest public concert ever,"
fuzzy aerial photographs of the mob and the aftermath, beer cans,
wine bottles, wrappers, while you sang, eyes closed, to her music.

If it wasn't Streisand, you played Wonder or El Combo—always music.
The Broadway classics you re-enacted from your director's chair:
*West Side Story, Godspell, JC Superstar,* with half a can
of root beer and a joint in the same hand, a lit Newport parked
in a garage-sale ashtray, and calla lilies that seemed to last forever
in candlelight umbra; the incense stick in the planter, almost out.

If there wasn't vodka there was usually dark rum. If not, we'd run out
to the Liquorvenient, talk small talk about clubs and Latin music
to the cashier. I'd flirt with her and get a 10% discount every time,
promising I'd pick her up later, and leave her bouncing in her chair
knowing I wouldn't be back, not for her, maybe for another six-pack
or bottle if we went dry—about 1:00 A.M., Enrique tapping empty cans

to a butter-knife salsa-beat and everyone waiting to use the can.
El Flaco *bongoing,* Maria *maracaing,* Roberto usually passed-out
in the air-conditioned back room—something like the Central Park
album scene—and you, *one-two-threeing* on clave, controlling the music,
orchestrating the mad dancing and singing from your usual chair,
in your Chinese-red slippers, the *Ghetto-Rican* in you, easy as ever,

with dubbed tapes, the 45s, the vinyl jewels you've kept forever
at arms reach. Nothing seemed to matter, not the spills or the cans,
the late rent, Kenita's health, the divorce, nor the broken dining chairs;
always a voice at 324, Elton or Puente, pop or Latin, blocking-out
the off-key howls as you wrote the soundtrack, the background music
of our lives—*merengued* worries; sung blues with Holliday in the dark.

Late night, we'd pack into one car to La Palma on *la ocho,* park
at the to-go window: *"seis* Cuban sandwiches." It took forever,
but the food was our kind, the place had a native charm, its own music:
the giant neon palm, the only place to get *Materva* in ice-cold cans
at that hour; the insomniac waitress, Nilda, her bouffant all puffed-out,
and riff-raff inside the restaurant *tequila'd-out* and numb in their chairs.

I still stop at La Palma when I can, at a sticky table with three chairs,
I drink espresso but remember the vodka, the music, Streisand singing out
in the middle of the park and our lives, as littered as they may be, forever.

## What Las Palmas Mean:

**I**

shade from moonlight
tango with a starry breeze

**II**

*café-con-leche* and pineapple soda
at *La Palma* take-out counter

**III**

the ghosts of the sand castles,
the sorceress of the coconut

**IV**

my gossiping ladies that tell no lies

**V**

the jagged edges of a parade
on a crowded, hot boulevard

**VI**

violins or bongos, on the sand—
we spill champagne or rum

**VII**

fuchsia neon No Vacancy flashing
at the Palms Motel—2:00 A.M.

## VIII

Martí: *las palmas son novias que esperan*

## IX

brides waltzing on the shore;
and the widows of the tropics

## X

P & S or VIVA CUBA
carved in block letters

## XI

the aphrodisiac of a people,
the talisman of a nation

## XII

swaying jade

## XIII

open hands—
broad and veined and still,
and still waiting.

# La Bella Dama of Little Havana

Mi Dama drags her plastic bags on past
los machos yelling *"Bella!"*—como locos
from Cuban coffee stands on Calle Ocho—
to count and crush her Coca-Cola cans,
and warn tramps of heaven's mighty plan.
Mi Dama, bare feet crossed, sits dressed in rojo,
the lights then dot and dress the streets in oro
while Dama makes her bed with paper ads.
La Bella Dama dreams of linen lunas,
another sky of rum and sugar clouds,
the Tropicana stars and silver plumas,
that lit Havana's midnight crowds—
her far city unmoved by dreams or pleas,
nor Dama's little bus bench memories.

## A Note About Sake

When I think of Manhattan, I think of Hiediki:
absorbed in a translation of Dostoevski,
reading back to front, left to right,
his loosened necktie sunk in the light
of that basement sake bar on Avenue B,
and interrupted by our drunk curiosity:
*how do you say "love" in Japanese?*
I think about the oriental girls too, tiny
vinyl purses swinging from thin cords,
mother-of-pearl combs scooping
vinyl black hair from giggling faces
as we rock-n-roll over the teak bar.

I remember the neon sheen and shows,
but still, I think of Hiediki most, how
far we were from our respective islands—
his fish and dragons, my sugar and congas.
And I'd like to believe we are whole,
despite the voids we fill with the familiar:
for Hiediki, the art of flowered sake bottles,
the balanced calligraphy of native letters,
the origami swans-a-swim by the register;
for me, a palm rustle, a swig of *café*
or of dark rum with lemon instead of
this warm wine with which we toast
to the pages of our unwritten biographies.

## The Silver Sands

Before the revival of quartz pinks and icy blues
on this neon beach of Art Deco hotels and boutiques,
there were the twilight verandas lined with retirees,
the cataract eyes of Mrs. Stein who would take us
for mezzanine bingo and pancakes at Wolfies;
I remember her beautiful orthopedic wobble.

Before sequined starlets popping out of limousine doors
and booze on the breath of every glitter-paved street,
there were the five-year-old summers of flamingo towels,
transistor radios blaring something in Spanish we ignored,
only curious of driftwood, washed-up starfish and jellyfish,
the beauty of broken conchs and our moated sand castles.

Before the widened sidewalks and pretentious cafés
where I take my cappuccino sprinkled with cinnamon,
our mothers were peacocks in flowered bathing caps
posing for sandy Polaroids like pageant contestants;
there were fifteen-cent Cokes to their ruby lips
and there was nothing their beauty couldn't conquer.

Before the demolition of the Silver Sands Hotel,
our fathers spun dominos under the thatch-palm gazebos,
drank then insulted the scenery: *Nada like our Varadero,*
*there the sand was powder; the water truly aquamarine.*
I remember the poor magic of those voices—
how beautifully they remembered beauty.

# Photo Shop

These faces are fifteen under faux diamond tiaras
and grandmother's smuggled *brillantes;*
these faces are pierced with the mango smiles
that dress hopeful *Teresitas* and *Marías*—
*quinceañeras* with coffee bean eyes;
these pearl faces are mother's taffeta dream,
a decorated anguish in painful pink manicures.
These young faces can't remember that last day—
the innocence of their small steps into the propeller
plane drifting above palms waving elegant farewells.
These barefoot faces are those red mountains
never climbed, a Caribbean never drunk,
they are a *guajiro* sugar never tasted.
These faces are displaced *Miritas* and *Susanitas.*
These faces are a 50s revolution
they are the Beatles and battles,
they are Celia Cruz—*AZUCAR*—loud and brown;
these faces rock-n-roll and roll their *r*'s,
they are eery *botánicas* and 7-Elevens.
These fiery faces are rifles and bongos,
they are *maracas* shaking, *machetes* hacking;
these faces carry too many names:
their white eyes are toppling dominos
their glossy eyes are rum and iced tea
their African eyes are gods and Castilian saints
haloed with the finest *tabaco* smoke.
These faces rest an entire ocean on Taino eyebrows;
they are Kennedy, Batista and Nixon,

they are a dragon in uniform;
these faces are singing two anthems,
nailed against walls, the walls are chipping.
These overflowing faces are swollen barrels
with rusting hoops and corset seams straining;
these faces are beans: black, red, white and blue,
with steaming rice on chipped china;
these faces are pork fat and lace gowns.
These standing faces are a sentinel—
when the Vietnamese kitchen next door stops
when the alley veils itself and closes like a fresh widow
when the flower shop draws in buckets of red carnations
when gold and diamonds are pulled from late windows
when neon flashes relieve the sun over these fading faces.
These chromatic faces are nothing important,
they are *nada* we need to understand,
they will transform in their photo chemistry,
these faces will collage very Americanly.

## Contemplations at the Virgin de la Caridad Cafetería, Inc.

*Que será, el café* of this holy, incorporated place,
the wild steam of scorched espresso cakes rising
like mirages from the aromatic waste, waving
over the coffee-glossed lips of these faces

assembled for a standing breakfast of nostalgia,
of tastes that swirl with the delicacy of memories
in these forty-cent cups of brown sugar histories,
in the swirling froth of *café-con-leche, que será,*

what have they seen that they cannot forget—
the broad-leaf waves of *tabaco* and plantains
the clay dust of red and nameless mountains,
*que será,* that this morning I too am a speck;

I am the brilliant guitar of a tropical morning
speaking Spanish and ribboning through potions
of waist-high steam and green cane oceans,
*que será,* drums vanishing and returning,

the African gods that rule a rhythmic land
playing their music: *bongó, bembé, conga;*
*que será,* that cast the spells of this *rumba,*
this wild birthright, this tropical dance

with the palms of this exotic confusion;
*que será,* that I too should be a question,
*que será,* what have I seen, what do I know—
culture of *café* and loss, this place I call home.

"En los montes, monte soy."
"Among the mountains, I am a mountain."

José Martí, *Versos Sencillos*

# Havanasis

In the beginning, before God created Cuba, the earth was chaos, empty of form and without music. The spirit of God stirred over the dark tropical waters and God said, "Let there be music." And a soft conga began a one-two beat in background of the chaos.

Then God called up *Yemayá* and said, "Let the waters under heaven amass together and let dry land appear." It was done. God called the fertile red earth Cuba and the massed waters the Caribbean. And God saw this was good, tapping his foot to the conga beat.

Then God said, "Let the earth sprout *papaya* and *coco* and white *coco* flesh; *malanga* roots and mangos in all shades of gold and amber; let their be *tabaco* and *café* and sugar for the *café;* let there be rum; let there be waving plantains and *guayabas* and everything tropical-like." God saw this was good, then fashioned palm trees—His pièce de résistance.

Then God said, "Let there be a moon and stars to light the nights over the Club Tropicana, and a sun for the 365 days of the year." God saw that this was good, he called the night nightlife, the day he called paradise.

Then God said, "Let there be fish and fowl of every kind." And there was spicy shrimp *enchilado,* chicken *fricasé,* codfish *bacalao* and fritters. But He wanted something more exciting and said, "Enough. Let there be pork." And there was pork—deep fried, whole roasted, pork rinds and sausage. He fashioned goats, used their skins for bongos and *batús;* he made *claves* and *maracas* and every kind of percussion instrument known to man.

Then out of a red lump of clay, God made a Taino and set him in a city He called *Habana.* Then He said, "It is not good that Taino be alone. Let me make him helpmates." And so God created the *mulata* to dance *guaguancó* and *son* with Taino; the *guajiro* to cultivate his land and his folklore, *Cachita* the sorceress to strike the rhythm of his music, and a poet to work the verses of their paradise.

God gave them dominion over all the creatures and musical instruments and said unto them, "Be fruitful and multiply, eat pork, drink rum, make music and dance." On the seventh day, God rested from the labors of his creation. He smiled upon the celebration and listened to their music.

## Varadero en Alba

**i.** *ven*

> *tus olas roncas murmuran entre ellas*
> *las luciérnagas se han cansado*
> *las gaviotas esperan como ansiosas reinas*

We gypsy through the island's north ridge
ripe with villages cradled in cane and palms,
the raw harmony of fireflies circling about
amber faces like dewed fruit in the dawn;

the sun belongs here, it returns like a soldier
loyal to the land, the leaves turn to its victory,
a palomino rustles its mane in blooming light.
I have no other vision of this tapestry.

**ii.** *ven*

> *tus palmas viudas quieren su danzón*
> *y las nubes se mueven inquietas como gitanas,*
> *adivina la magia encerrada del caracol*

The morning pallor blurs these lines:
horizon with shore, mountain with road;
the shells conceal their chalky magic,
the dunes' shadows lengthen and grow;

I too belong here, sun, and my father
who always spoke paradise of the same sand
I now impress barefoot on a shore I've known
only as a voice held like water in my hands.

### iii.    *ven*

> *las estrellas pestañosas tienen sueño*
> > *en la arena, he grabado tu nombre,*
> > > *en la orilla, he clavado mi remo*

There are names chiseled in the ivory sand,
striped fish that slip through my fingers
like wet and cool ghosts among the coral,
a warm rising light, a vertigo that lingers;

I wade in the salt and timed waves,
facing the losses I must understand,
staked oars crucifixed on the shore.
Why are we nothing without this land?

# The Road to Rancho Luna

Darkness rises out of darkness, what light exists
is thickened with the ambrosia of tropical fog—
splintered wood farmhouses and pinto horses,
in silent prayer of clearings marked by fence lines,
every silhouette and its shadow, a double dark.

The moonlight pulls shadows, we disturb
the unanimous black, the democratic dark
with the clatter and rust of a Soviet sedan rushed
by vigil images in dream motion of *el camposanto*
impressing us with a vague understanding.

The implicit secrets of that deep, deep green
where we too have been only images to one another,
forms, victims of artifice, of time and space,
of the divisions of political and geographical lines
now intersecting at a point east of the crescent bay.

At Rancho Luna cove we learn a common language,
we delve in the coarseness of sand dunes,
in the smoothness of native rum and slow waves
setting the rhythm of humid breaths we sculpt
into words that carve our faces out of darkness.

Eye to eye, we see the common genetic geometry—
*comunista* or *capitalista*—we agree to write often,
then turn to the dim road, the moon full witness
to the pact of our light-filled footprints
shimmering, eroding, vanishing on the shore.

## Havana 50s

The ghost songs linger under boomerang tiers
and the chipping mosaics of *El Habana Hilton,*
echoes of boleros swaying in the dull chandeliers
the tropical dust of *merengue, conga,* and *son*.
*Contradanza,* cocktails, and corsages at El Caprí,
rumba, rayon shirts, La Lupe singing at La Red,
*montuno,* mink stoles, and Moré at Sans Souci,
the *Cuba Libre* buzz, the back door wide open;
the rhinestone cabarets featuring feathered girls
in a third world dancing away from the moon,
shifting their hips to conga beats and the rifles
hidden and polished high in the red mountains—
*Life*'s cover—25 cents for the triumph of Castro
while Connecticut housewives do the mambo.

# El Jagua Resort

Cienfuegos Bay encroaches on the city,
its cankerous seawall carves out the shape
of an unlucky horseshoe fastened
with the remains of colonial *viviendas*
still standing like scoured sand castles,
conquered faces peering from behind
famished columns, stucco revealing
a cryptic history in decades of chipped
cyan blue and Spanish red layers.

The *special* buses from Havana
arrive at Cienfuegos every Tuesday.
Smoked in black diesel, they deliver
batches of pale tourists in white linen
to *El Jagua,* a preserved 1950s resort,
where Canadians and Italians step out
drunk congas from megaphone instructions—
side-to-side, kick-then-kick, hand-to-hip;
caught in spells of *tabaco,* dark rum,
brown sugar, and the young *mulatas*
who tempt the married men not like
bitches or feathered whores but like
a sea wind singing through wind chimes.
Scents of *dólares* and *dolores* around
the cracked plaster of the pool bar.

Iliana is sixteen with expired papers,
hungry and documented as "uncooperative."
Tangoed in a crepe of borrowed silk,
she dances with the ricochets of her dark curls,
promotes her *canela* flesh and crescent lips.
Iliana scatters like cinnamon powder in
the revolving eclipses over the fanned bar;
evaporates like a brush of perfume
into the inelegant lap of a French *canadiense*
whose elegant name she cannot nasal.
As Alejandro serves Habana Club & Coke—
*Cuba Libre*—for quarter tips, Iliana decides
on how many bars of laundry soap
or black market trinkets to charge, hoping
he will want to pay her in cash.

Nightfalls are abrupt at *El Jagua,* not
the adagio witchcraft of harvest moonrises
but a quick drum slap in tandem with
the iron door slam of oceanview #634—
the tempest of Iliana naked and recanting
her faith in the lamp-light gods of her bedside;
and the opaque gods glowing from within
the strung flesh of gaping snapper mouths;
and the barefoot gods that dine on sugarwater
and sell silver pompoms of stitched fish;
and the capsized mouths of sea gods
bobbing in a poisoned bay without antidote;
and the gods hidden inside the splintered hulls
of moonlit dinghies and withered coconuts;

the gods that pull voices out of the harbor,
the gods that brew the rain and cut the cane,
the green gods that possess the palm trees;
the blaze of all the gods burning here
in this great city of a hundred fires.

## Last Night in Havana

Drifting from above, the palms seem to sink
willingly into the saffron ground, all I can map
is the marble veins of rivers turning static,
the island coastline retreating like a hem
from the sargasso patches of Caribbean.
I think of you *primo,* huddled on the edge
of an Almendares curb last night,
El Greco shadow spilt across the street,
and over the tracks stapled to the weeds
below your open bedroom window.
Covered in cobwebs of humid wind,
we slapped at unreachable mosquitos
as Havana's tenements collapsed around us,
enclosed us like the yellow of old books
or the stucco walls of a hollow chapel.
You confessed you live ankled in the sand
of a revolution, watching an unparted sea,
marking tides and learning currents
that will carry you through the straits
to my door, blistered and salted, but alive.
You said you want silence, you want to leave
the sweep of the labor trains in your window,
the creak of your father's wheelchair in the hall
searching for a bottle of pills he will find empty,
and the slam of your eyelids forcing sleep.
The tires are ready, bound with piano wire,

the sail will be complete with the linen scraps
your mother will stitch together after midnights
when the neighbors are trying to fall asleep.
Last night in Havana, your face against your knees,
your words drowning with the lees in an empty bottle
of bootleg wine you clutched around the neck
and will keep to store fresh water.

## El Juan

Juan, meet with neighbors.
Juan, meet with strangers.
Juan, tie wire and truck tires.
Juan, take your oars and rosary.
Juan, leave the necklace of palms.
Juan, supplicant of the sea.
Juan, bastard of the sun.
Juan, of salt and blistered lip.
Juan, of bloated feet and fingers.
Juan, this is your sacrament.
Juan, fold your hands and pray:
*in the name of your father, of your sons,*
*and of your holy virgin of the sea.*

# Partial List: Guantánamo Detainees

No. 4352C Castillo, Carlos Armando, b. 1952, Cienfuegos, hijo de Angela y Juan

No. 4441P Córdova, Jorge Luis, b. 1941, Habana, busca a su primo Fernando González

No. 4558H Cortéz, Emilia de la Caridad, b. 1958, Pinal del Río, busca a su hermano Ramón Pérez

No. 4690S Cruz, Alberto Ignacio, b. 1980, Santa Clara, RELEASED

No. 4755M Capt. Cruz, Enrique Manuel, b. 1955, Mariel, con hijos Roberto y Elizabeth

No. 4846H De León, Ana Patricia, b. 1946, Habana, hija de Gabriela y Ernesto

No. 4932S Delgado, María del Carmen, b. 1952, RELEASED

No. 5038H Díaz, Antonio Eduardo, b. 1938, Habana, busca a su hermana, Ana Fernández

No. 5155V Díaz, Jorge Enrique, b. 1955, Varadero, a busca su madre, Elena María

No. 5247H Díaz, Pedro Geraldo, b. 1947, Habana, busca a su padre, Raúl

# FOUND LETTERS FROM 1965: EL AÑO
# DE LA AGRICULTURA

**I.**   Received by my mother from her sister,
December 1, 1965, Cienfuegos, Cuba

*"A brief letter which perhaps may be the last,*
*now that we have each chosen different paths.*
*I understand you are definitely leaving."*

The glorious seventh year of *la Revolución*,
unanimously declared the year of AGRICULTURA,
the State decrees the harvests must double.
Whichever generous goddess may be,
*el espíritu*—the one deity in the rock
of this island who chose the *guajiro,*
and listens to *machete* prayers, listened:
out of red earth rose the canes, rose the corn;
thousands of coffee-bean eyes—the mountains saw,
the valleys yawned mouthfuls of mangos.

*"Why, what else do you need, food? Not even.*
*You have arroz and frijoles criollos;*
*true, they were expensive, but . . ."*

tons of sweetening *azúcar*
tons of enlivening *café*
tons of tempting *mangos*—
exports for the foreign palate,
while they let you eat *arroz y frijoles*

*"I never thought you would make such a decision,*
*since you have never been endangered by la Revolución."*

The same glorious year, the visas arrive
with the brand of a *contra-revolucionaria*.
Like the harvest, now you begin to double
into one who leaves, and one who remains.
The hands that want to leave are tired
of soaking beans, stealing sugar from the mill,
boiling vats of rice pudding for tired mouths
forced to greet friends with *"hola compañero,"*
forced to swallow the vinegar of citizen patrols.
The ears leave the whispers and speeches,
the hammer of machine guns and promises;
The eyes that want to close and run, sleep open,
against the required glossy of El Comandante,
his neoclassical hand lifted above you.
*Bendito Hermes, Mercurio, Eleguá—*
all gods of *los caminos*—guide you,
the hands, the ears, the eyes that leave.

*"And now you so easily leave all your possessions*
*to your enemy—el Gobierno."*

The State allows one suitcase, take anything except:
your *Quinces* pin, diamond chips set in plated gold—

## PROPERTY OF THE STATE

the wedding rings and Catholic saint charms,
an *azabache* pendant to protect against evil spirits—

## PROPIEDAD DEL ESTADO

your *pesos cubanos* and your child's toys, gracias—

## DONATIONS TO THE STATE

nudes of your son on the dresser splashing violet water,
you, posed coyly in chin-high pants mated against a palm,
black-and-white images of your husband in uniform peeling
from the black pages of construction paper photo albums—

## MEMORIES OF THE STATE

But you search for a way to smuggle the perfume—
one part smoke of sugarcane cuttings smoldering,
two parts spray of citrus split open with incisive fingers,
one part rainfall evaporating and cane juice boiling;
three parts the rum *décimas* of *guajiro* guitars
four parts fields of mild winter skies seeded with stars—
an *eau de toilette* for pulses at the wrists and temples
on foreign days when you will have no language,
only the intimacy of memory's scents.

*"In a strange country, you may have all you need . . .*
*at the price of being separated from your family*
*which you know you will never see again."*

Primo Felipe, Tía Delia, Claudia Pérez your neighbor,
your sisters: Gloria, Tania, Alina; Rodríguez the baker;
Tío José, your brother Sergio, and your *Mamá*—

FAMILY OF THE STATE

II.      My mother's reply to her sister,
         December 10, 1965, Cienfuegos, Cuba

*"I have chosen no path, I am simply fulfilling*
*the destiny my life affords me."*

At the end of the glorious *año* you take
the road curling away from your town,
the sugarcane fields transform into a farewell of mirrors
reflecting all the images you will never see again:
the mill clock, the reservoir, raw sugar in your hands,
*your* clouds, *your* moon, moving over *your* land
of polished fruits ripening on the branch,
of palm tree rustle and shadows on the ground,
of coconuts hatching in a splash of splinters.
You remember your mother's eye gestures,
powdering your cheeks, penciling your eyebrows;
your father at a bowl of hot cornmeal,
eating in the dignity and good silence of your home.

*"The ideas and concepts which bind family should*
*reign above all other concepts, religious or political."*

You reach Havana for the last time,
the mirrors recede—*el fin* of your life's reel,

a sea of still tarmac spread before you,
and a set of stairs leading into the airplane's belly.
Everything coalesces to a point, the projection
of all the gods of *la Revolución,* all the harvests,
all the years add up to the moment you cross
the platform and look back one last time
to face the retreating template of the island,
and scribble relatives' names, birth dates,
addresses, your favorite poems and flowers—
convinced that you will forget these things.
The propeller blades hum suicidally, you pause
to scan lines of the letter you've written,
the same letter I now find, thirty years later,

for lies:
*"At no time have political concepts*
*influenced my decision to leave my country . . ."*

for fears:
*"In a strange country the future is unknowable . . .*
*will I lose those I leave behind . . ."*

for courage:
*"I hurt at the thought of separating from all of you and Mamá,*
*but I have chosen a husband, I have united my life,*
*together, our destiny leads us to another country . . ."*

repeat it:
*"together, our destiny leads us to another country.*
*I am not the first nor the last woman*
*to do such a thing."*

## The Reservoir

**I**

Clamor of rail cars, the labor of gears,
the mystery of sugar crystalizing in vats

spinning clockwise at the speed of light,
centrifugal forces pulling into focus

a photo memory of you in chin pants,
in an S-shape pose, fresh hip tilted left,

the organic lines of your 1965 body
curled and matted by the jagged shade,

the stiff palms staked along the banks
of the reservoir—dammed potential

ready for the draw from the mill,
and your potent youth ready to power

the mechanics of the grinding years
ahead that would consume you.

**II**

Chemical images, the Technicolor
of the mountains that rose behind you,

now rises behind me, the same valley,
twin palms and grassy slopes where

I pose with the vapor of my solitude;
the mill exhales steam, time whistles,

the entire world deaf, past and present
skimming over the reservoir's surface.

## Abuela Valdés

The day is rich, the graves are simple,
not the regalia of Colón in La Habana,
but equal dignity exists here at Palmira,
whose name translates into a view of palms.
Among the palms, also sugar, gossip, witchcraft;
a land, a body, and a name I never learned—
Claudia Molina Valdés—the grandmother
who remained here, refracted by seawater.

Now you are a Braille touch of chiseled granite,
letters and numbers rub against my fingers,
into the alphabet of a recurring dream:
I am blind in flight through razored leaves
of sugarcane stalks in fields of endless cutting
carrying accented vowels in crystal bowls.
Congas beat strong consonants against
mangos that ripen and rot on the branch;
a shadow passes over a bare mountain
and your syllables flee like startled birds
dispersed by graveyard bells, your eyes open
like strawberries, wrinkled in a photo of you
mother has kept on her dresser, a dusted place
to arrange flowers with your absence.

And the flowers are roses without lament
that wither into the open letter of 1972,

careful writing announcing your death.
I've known you only as a word, letters
I've tossed like ebony coins into the air
anticipating the flat vision of your face.

# El Cucubano

Lucía enjoyed the mystery, the emerald light
captive in the bright belly of *los cucubanos*
she wore clipped to her home-sewn dress
parading like a peacock at the town socials
around the reservoir and sugar mill clock.
All the señoritas flashed their *cucubanos*—
live pendants adorning breasts and hearts
to compete with the swirl of *guajiro* stars
for the attention of prime young caballeros
in linen *guayaberas* and straw hats;
the clock chiming every hour of courting,
denying every second of lustful thought
in the smolders of raped sugarcane fields.

Lucía knew nothing of the nerve stimulations,
the reactions that produced the bound light
of balanced chemicals in glowing abdomens.
What she knew was how the male *cucubanos*
tracked females by following their flashes;
how to trap them in her mother's glass jars
in the hours of the early evening before
the moon rises strong and snuffs their glow;
how to pinch them so they cling to the dress,
near the heart, calling attention to the breasts,
the green fire silhouetting the spell of nipples.

Lucía never questioned the cool light nor Alberto
when he took her, removed her *cucubano,*
said she wouldn't be needing fireflies anymore
now that she'd belong to him and his promises.
Lucía knows how *el cucubano* swirled away
from Alberto's fingers into infinite green spirals
through palm trees and mountains, how soon after
the harvest Alberto also disappeared.
Lucía stares at stars she swears are green,
traps *cucubanos* between her cupped hands,
jade oozing between the seams of her fingers,
the phenomenon of luminescence in her palms—
light without heat, love without love.

## Zafra

During the October *zafra,* smoking brick stacks
spew a warm snow of *bagazo* cinders unto
rail lines that disappear into the churn of the mill—
the mechanical dragon of steam and sputter
is fed the hacked sweetness of cane-filled *carretas.*
At two o'clock, for a hundred years
*macheteros* like Tío Chilo from the fields,
with throbbing forearm and soaked cotton,
return to the smells of their sunlit homes,
to wood ovens and grease blackened *cazuelas.*
The jewels harvested from the red dust rotate
from hand to hungry hand, from land to mouth,
while machetes glint and mark time staked
like sundials in the abandoned clearings.

# The Morning Kill

The morning was unusually mild for May,
and that scraping was the sound of the men
sharpening dull knives with other dull knives,
shooting warm *añejo* rum for courage,
and inspecting the glint of fresh steel
against the sunlight that disturbed my sleep.
In the dank and dark comfort of my corral
on a good bed of straw and moist, cool mud,
there, I rested knowing nothing.

They did with me as they did with the others,
a swift stab behind the left leg, to the heart,
but they missed, one of the men
had put his hand into me and yanked at it
then the blood blurted out in a red scream,
rivered down the center of the pathway
where the vampire flies are now drinking
greedily at the edges of the puddled blood,
before the sun evaporates their meal.

I remember their surgeon red hands
that had wrestled me to the ground,
the tribal paint streaks down their cheeks
when they wiped sweat from their faces,
the sweet rum in the laughter of their mockery—
now what *¡Ahora que machote!*—

now when I had weakened, they watched
the slowing heaves of my chest waiting
for the last breath, my murder, their meal.

I should've known this morning,
the way the women had kitchen-fussed,
the clanging cauldrons of boiling well water
they are now using to soften and shave away
my skin from its flaccid, castrated body.
For the first time I watch from above them,
they're peeling fat, stripping guts—
that heart of mine, that liver of mine,
such a delicate and beautiful arrangement.

I know I've lived well and with honor
for today there will be a feast in my name,
you will all sleep full for weeks to come
from the rest of this morning's kill,
at each meal, you will remember me.

# Tía Olivia Serves Wallace Stevens a Cuban Egg

The ration books voided, there was little to eat,
so Tía Olivia ruffled four hens to serve Stevens
a fresh *criollo* egg. The singular image lay limp,
floating in a circle of miniature roses and vines
etched around the edges of the rough dish.
The saffron, inhuman soul staring at Stevens
who asks what yolk is this, so odd a yellow?

Tell me Señora, if you know, he petitions,
what exactly is the color of this temptation:
I can see a sun, but it is not the color of suns
nor of sunflowers, nor the yellows of Van Gogh,
it is neither corn nor school pencil, as it is,
so few things are yellow, this, even more precise.

He shakes some salt, eye to eye hypothesizing:
a carnival of hues under the gossamer membrane,
a liqueur of convoluted colors, quarter-part orange,
imbued shadows, watercolors running a song
down the spine of praying stems, but what, then,
of the color of the stems, what green for the leaves,
what color the flowers; what of order for our eyes
if I can not name this elusive yellow, Señora?

Intolerant, Tía Olivia bursts open Stevens's yolk,
plunging into it with a sharp piece of Cuban toast:
It is yellow, she says, *amarillo y nada más, bien?*

The unleashed pigments begin to fill the plate,
overflow onto the embroidered place mats,
stream down the table and through the living room
setting all the rocking chairs in motion then
over the mill tracks cutting through cane fields,
a viscous mass downing palm trees and shacks.

In its frothy wake whole choirs of church ladies
clutch their rosary beads and sing out in Latin,
exhausted *macheteros* wade in the stream,
holding glinting machetes overhead with one arm;
*cafeteras,* '57 Chevys, uniforms and empty bottles,
mangy dogs and fattened pigs saved from slaughter,
Soviet jeeps, *Bohemia* magazines, park benches,
all carried in the egg lava carving the molested valley
and emptying into the sea. *Yellow,* Stevens relents,
Yes. But then what the color of the sea, Señora?

## Décima Guajira

### I

*Veo la tierra amada*
*los pasos de mis padres*
*dentro estos muertos ojos*
*ahora baila y canta*
*el azúcar, la décima.*

The *guajiro* arias of *la décima* drift
in the lifted dust of brackish shadows
over dancing sugarcane that follows
the meter, the rhyme, the ten-line craft
of my grandfather's melancholy gift.

### II

*Bajo tu manta de polvo*
*aquí encuentro y guardo*
*mi alma tallada en mármol*
*como un talismán de caracol*
*que guardo en la mano.*

It is this mantle of dust that keeps
the marble music, the drifting sand
of footprints blown over this loved land;
the talismans in the hands of my sleep
that sing so slow and so very deep.

# Postcard to W. C. Williams from Cienfuegos

On the other side of these words
are the tender green cane fields-
my sugar, my alcohol, my rum—
the chartreuse just after the rain.

This is *my* green wheelbarrow,
beauty, compelled by verdure,

even the white roses in my head
burn jealous in a candle flicker—

petals turn and coil in the flame,
blacken to a foil of happy ash
that scatters among the palms.

## Palmita Mía

Así eres:
la palma libre
        de mi reposo,
la lluvia inquieta
        de tus ramas
el río que reuno
        en mis manos
y llevo a este
        labio inútil,
tú, mi sed y mi agua
        mi sombra tranquila.

Así eres:
isla larga y espigada
        contigo me estiro
mi espalda se rompe
        contra tus costas.
eres el exilio
        de mi exilio,
eres la montaña roja,
        el valle cálido
es mi boca abierta
        esperando tu cosecha.

Así eres:
la cuna verde
        el pulso
disuelto en la mano,
        un corazón de colibrí
y el centinela de estrellas,
        atenta fe
entre palmas rezando
        un credo a la brisa:
vino de coco, pan de arena
        palmita mía.

## Palmita Mía

     You are this:
the free palm
     of my rest,
the impatient rain
     from your fronds
a river I collect
     in my open hands
and bring to my dry
     useless lip,
you, my thirst, my water
     my tranquil shade.

     You are this:
the drawn island lean
     I stretch with you,
my back breaks
     against your coast,
you are the exile
     of my exile
you are the red mountain,
     the temperate valley
is my mouth open
     waiting for your harvest

You are this:
the green crib
      the pulse
loose in open hand,
      a hummingbird heart
and the sentinel of still stars,
      attentive faith
among the praying palms,
      a creed of breezes:
coconut wine, loaves of sand,
      *palmita mía.*

# Acknowledgments / Agradecimientos

Grateful acknowledgment is made to the following publications in which some of the poems in this collection first appeared, some in slightly different form: *Amelia* ("324 Mendoza, #6," "La Bella Dama of Little Havana," and "Havana 50s"); *America's Review* ("Teatro Martí"); *Excursus Literary Journal* ("324 Mendoza, #6" and "Contemplations at the Virgin de la Caridad Cafetería, Inc."); *Fashion Spectrum* ("The Silver Sands"); *Generation Ñ* ("Photo Shop"); *Gulfstream Magazine* ("La Revolución at Antonio's Mercado"); *Having a Wonderful Time, an Anthology of South Florida Writers,* Simon & Schuster ("El Malibú"); *Indiana Review* ("Teatro Martí" and "Tía Olivia Serves Wallace Stevens a Cuban Egg"); *Latino Stuff Review* ("La Revolución at Antonio's Mercado" and "Teatro Martí"); *Little Havana Blues,* an anthology of Cuban-American writers, Arte Público Press ("Mail for Mamá," "América," and "Crayons for Elena"); *Luna* ("Palmita Mía" and "El Malibú"); *Michigan Quarterly Review* ("Havanasis" and "The Silver Sands"); *The Nation* ("Last Night in Havana"); *Post Modern Notes* ("Mail for Mamá"); *Quince Magazine* ("Photo Shop"); *Tri-Quarterly* ("Mango, Number 61"); *VOX* ("Letter to El Flaco on His Birthday").

This page allows me the opportunity to thank those who are essential to my voice: my family—Geysa, Caco, Chichi—and good friends—Sonia, Carlos, Alberto, Darden, and Nikki. You are what is good and beautiful. Also, Sandra Castillo, Dan Wakefield, and especially Campbell McGrath for his unique gifts as educator and friend. But above all, Christina Rivera, who dreamed a dream for me.

En esta página tengo la oportunidad de agradecer a aquellas personas esenciales que me han dado vida y voz: mi familia—Geysa, Caco, Chichi—y buenas amistades—Sonia, Carlos, Alberto, Darden, y Nikki. Ustedes son lo que es bueno y bello. También, Sandra Castillo, Dan Wakefield, y especialmente Campbell McGrath por sus dones únicos como educador y amigo. Pero sobre todo, Christina Rivera, quien soñó mi sueño.

*photo: Carlos Betancourt*

**Richard Blanco** was made in Cuba, assembled in Spain, and imported to the United States—meaning his mother, seven months pregnant, and the rest of the family arrived as exiles from Cienfuegos, Cuba, to Madrid, where he was born. Only forty-five days later, the family emigrated once more and settled in New York City, then eventually in Miami where he was raised and educated. His resumé and interests are as diverse and read as colorfully as his background: professional engineer, translator, furniture designer, YMCA volunteer, underwater photographer, bongo player, and salsa dancer. Blanco has been featured as guest poet on the National Public Radio show *All Things Considered*, and his work has appeared in *The Nation, Indiana Review, Michigan Quarterly, TriQuarterly Review,* and several anthologies. A builder of bridges and poems, Blanco received both a Bachelor of Science degree in civil engineering (1991) and a Master in Fine Arts in creative writing (1997) from Florida International University. He works as a consultant engineer and writes from his home on the ocean in Miami Beach, where he is currently working on his next book of poems.